Boundless 2015

V.I.P.F.

The Anthology of the Rio Grande Valley International Poetry Festival

Edited by Daniel García Ordaz

McAllen, Texas

Rio Grande Valley International Poetry Festival
www.valleypoetryfest.org

Boundless is the official anthology of the Rio Grande Valley
International Poetry Festival, a program of Art That Heals, Inc.

Published by El Zarape Press: McAllen TX USA

Boundless 2015: Poetry-American. Poetry—World.
Poetry—Anthology.
A collection of poetry by poets from the United States, Europe,
Latin America, and Asia. Edited by Daniel García Ordaz.
Cover photograph (Botanical Gardens, Balboa Park, San Diego)
by Gina M. García
ISBN-10: 0-9789954-3-0
ISBN-13: 978-0-9789954-3-0

Cover design by Daniel García Ordaz, El Zarape Press
Printed in the United States of America.

DEDICATION

To the poets of the Rio Grande Valley and our fellow poets from
across Texas and the United States and the world.
In honor of

Jan Seale, 2012 Texas Poet Laureate

In memoriam:

Dr. Gloria E. Anzaldúa

Jovita González

Dr. Américo Paredes

Raúl R. Salinas

Trinidad Sánchez, Jr.

CONTENTS

ACKNOWLEDGMENTS

With grateful acknowledgement to El Zarape Press, The McAllen Chamber of Commerce, the Mission Historical Museum, Paragraphs On Padre, and Art That Heals, Inc.

Daniel García Ordaz and Brenda Nettles Riojas
Founders

Holding a Book Before Reading
Shirley Rickett

This book looks long.
Its cover shines with promise.
So many words in narrow channels
lined up like children waiting
for lunch or recess in school.
It will be milk money collected
and the hall monitors moving
like small ships in the old dark halls.
There will be the smell of those
ancient oaken floors, their creak
and the sound of my sixth grade
teacher's shoes on the boards,
her run up the wide stairs.

And there will be pain almost
too hard to bear and it will fade
to nothing in one day.
It will return on other pages
at the playground, the fall
off the jungle-gym, the looks
of the child I told the joke to
I'd heard my father repeat
with its embedded swear words
and the listener recoiled and left me,
and the lines of dirt on my neck
where I hadn't washed while
my mother went to the hospital
to birth my brother through agony
left behind from my own breech birth.
This book looks long.

I Found A Poet
César Leonardo De León

I found a poet at the coffee shop.
He hadn't slept for years.
His blood was being used
        to spike weak espressos.

I found a poet at the beach.
She blessed and cursed the waves
            for their impermanence.

I found a poet at the bus stop.
            The roses on her skirt made
            an old man smile as she walked past him.

I found another on my broken tongue
That reclaims conquered words
        like chocolate and mesquite.

I found one
in the darkest corner of my room
        where nightmares sleep.

I found several at the bar,
several inside the church,
several in offices, and behind desks
        writing secret stanzas.

I found Some by the river,
        Some on roads.

So many poets.
So many words.
So many verses.
So many universes.
        So little time.

The Slums In Our Heads
Odilia Galván Rodríguez

born in poverty
from Texas to Illinois
played barefoot in dirt

red-earth gave us dignity
we didn't know we were poor
except for the lash

passed down the generations
that was the man's best weapon,
we stomping our own

saved on nooses, bullets,
those pox blankets - moth eaten and
too thread bare to sell

as we grew-up we learned well
to whip ourselves into line
self-hatred a built in sentry

we gave ourselves
away ~ not buying our own beauty
reaping seeds of hate

sown in bloodied fields
of greed called freedom, but not
for us – to toil in

we came complete
with ticking time bombs ready
to go off on ourselves

we accept our fate unwillingly
knowing there are other truths
to be told deep, by sweet river's edge

we must sing back ancestral memory
from before their time moved on
before the reign of terror
        left slums buried in our heads

I Have No Estate
Linda Romero

I have no estate, no
Self-made life of home,
Baby keepsakes or heirlooms
Given in marriage to leave
Behind – no children to pass
On memories of when I wore Papi's
Hat and pretended to play guitar;
Sat on Grandpa's lap with stories
Of bunnies in Spanish, and pictures
Of me in my red and white batter's
Uniform; tunas grew on the cactus
And I played in dirt in my Sunday dress
But I have my words – undisciplined
Journal entries of young, unrequited
Love, struggles with math in college
And learning differences; to get anywhere,
One must struggle along the way.
But sharing joy is invaluable.

Cuisine De Your 'Hood
Eduardo R. Vega

I saw a Chipotle billboard that read "Cuisine de your 'hood"
Needless to say I was initially excited
Though, as I went in, I was sorely disappointed.
You see, first of all, no one in my 'hood ever used the word
"cuisine"
If I had ever mentioned that word, I would likely have heard
"¿Qué es eso?" "¿Cui - qué?" or "¡Cochino!"
But more importantly, they didn't have
anything that my mom prepared for us, back in our "hood"

Fresh flour tortillas with butter, or fresh corn tortillas with
salt, or
A slice of bologna, warmed on the comál, thrown into a
tortilla of any kind
Macaroni and cheese, with weenies chopped up and thrown
in
Spam
Fideo from the yellow box
Hamburger Helper
Chicken Helper
or if it was Lent, Tuna Helper
tamales, lightly fried, with chili con carne and a slice of
processed cheese on top
weenie and egg tacos
4/$1 frozen burritos from HEB
Or the combination pizza from the deli section that had
pepperoni in tiny cubes

I didn't realize then,
that our 'hood was so humble

You see, we didn't eat like royalty
But when my mother put a plate in front of me,
I felt like a prince

So Chipotle people,
Just because you serve stuff in tortillas and sprinkle white
cheese on it
Doesn't mean you know what I ate in my 'hood
Having carnitas on your menu doesn't mean you're
authentic
And honestly, we never put chicken or steak on a bed of
romaine lettuce
(I didn't see romaine lettuce until college)

Yeah, I'll still visit y'all, but not because of any sort of
nostalgia

I like your burritos.

The Importance of Girls
Shawna Kennedy

The boy smiles across the room at a girl, who in turn
 flips her hair cause she sees him looking.
When he sees her flipping
it's important to him,
 because it means
he's worth a flip
to someone,
anyone.

She gets in trouble with the teacher for not listening
and it's true, that she's listening to someone else,
but it's just as important to her
to her self-worth to
be heard by the boy
wearing the blue
striped shirt.

His clothes are the same as the day before, yesterday's
stains,
on today's T- shirt. He's holding onto another, to change
into after P.E., after his shower of the day.
She doesn't notice it, doesn't care,
she just smiles at him
and flips her hair.

She smiles and looks down when she answers questions
but attempts acts of bravery, in front of him.
Her head up, cutting her eyes over smiles
when she reads her answers,
his boyish approval
is all she wants
so he smiles
she flips
her hair.

Turning The Other Cheek
Lisa Adam

It's the moment before the second blow
that will mark you most,

the brief suspension
between violence and violence,

the involuntary inhalation of breath,
the eerie sunshine calm at the eye of the storm

when you look out and instantly apprehend
the twisted wreckage

and you know it's not over: the slam
of the towering eye wall is returning.

It doesn't make you meek; it makes you strong.
It makes you brace yourself, and batten down
the doors and windows of your soul.

Her Tree Branches Dance In Rain
Joanne Uppendahl

Though
she suffers,
never think
of Earth as dead:
birds drift and murmur
at dusk,
sending her stories
to mountain ridges.

Her seas
are like saucepans,
simmering
with ginger light,
filled with
foaming life.

Take one clear look:
you will see
her grace
covering
mountain crests,
amethyst deeps
of canyons.

All her tree branches
dance in rain;
her bunched clouds
are pregnant
with bolts of lightning.

Wind
breathes
her aliveness
into your lungs,

even now.

Spilling Poetry
Lucinda Zamora-Wiley

I was busy planting silent poems
in my head.
Every slash of white on the black
highway suggested punctuation marks
to suit metaphors and similes.

There were question marks
in constellations,
semicolons in barbed wire fences,
and periods pelted
my windows. But this was no ordinary
syncopation . . .

A swarm of lightning bugs painted
themselves on the canvas of my windshield,
splashes of electric-green luminescence
to light up a nighttime Jackson Pollack.

But theirs was temporary genius . . . their masterpiece was
erased as quickly as it was shone.
I was the only audience —
no crowd to appreciate their life's sacrifice
of fading, glowing glory.

I see that this is my poem
making its mark . . . and missing it, too.
Lighting the world for a fleeting, flying moment,
of family and beating wings.

We are all poets slamming into windshields
paying for words in blood,
punctuating experience in amber and bronze,
all that throbs and oozes out of
our hearts, the fleshy parts of us, an offering.

Long after we are gone,
our blood will speak for us.

Ten Minutes
Laura Peña

My cluttered office
has pieces of furniture
crammed against the walls.
Books of poets known nationally
and known only here in Texas
stand side by side
on the shelves like sentinels.
My dog lies on the futon.
Notebooks, pens, papers,
occupy every inch of space.
Stuffed under the weight
of *Writer's Kits* and journals
my early stories — I have not
read them in decades.
Is that my voice?
That shy girl afraid to show
those adolescent longings?
My coffee mug sits with a few dregs
of coffee grounds and sparkles of cinnamon.
How I like to sweeten it instead of sugar.
How to spend these last ten minutes?
My husband said with someone
he loves — not writing.
But writing is what I do.
I would spend my last
ten minutes with him
a pen in my hand
writing on our arms and legs.
Maybe the blast
will tattoo the ink
under our skins
and we'll be hung
on the ruins.

A Forest Of Shadows
Mario Mansilla Moya

Not knowing how I got there,
I started wandering around.
It was autumn, I could tell by the air
and because the leaves were all colored brown.
By a cypress tree, I laid,
and woke up by a scream of aid.
It was already late night
and Zeus had made his way into the sky.
As I looked for the stranger,
I was caught by a great danger:
between the thunder and the lightning,
a countless number of shadows started sparkling.
I kept walking terrified
and this evil chase became a delight,
so when I found whoever for help screamed,
I told him, "Do not fear this is just like a dream."
But when he saw me, his face turned pale
and then ran as if he did from hell.
Disappointed, I sat on the ground
as the shadows gathered in a circle around.
And then in my head began a dwell:
Am I one of these shadows as well?

Night Voices
Joanne Uppendahl

Sprouting inside her breast
within her tenderest flesh

into milk glands that gave
inexhaustible provisions

a lump is growing as if
to deny her right to live

her life of motherhood
of friends and teaching

soft night voices whisper
calling from stars to Earth

angels of hope and healing
of comfort, love and light:

do not despair, sweet child,
for we dwell by your side.

Lasting Moments
Nianna E. Gustovich

These are lasting moments
We will always share.
I'll remember the poem you read . . .
And you were sitting in that chair.

He sang a song he wrote
While she sipped her coffee.
Another played all the notes.
You just sat and nodded.

The bearded Walt Whitman
Said "In vino veritas"
And quaffed a fourth copa
Prepping himself for pizzazz.

The girlfriends tapped their acrylics
Bidding their friends
Come join them for an evening
Of social fun that never ends.

You see a cup, a table, a chair,
A guy in holey blue jeans
A hippie, a dandy,
Some who live above their means.

I, however, see so much more
Than a group of people
Seated in a coffee shop.
I see essence like a needle,

A vaccine of life
For the community in which we live,

A virus of creativity
To foster and to give.

You are the memory.
You breathe the wind.
You live the moment
In my mind that you will transcend.

¡Auxilio!
Nephtalí De León

ella gritaba
corriendo por su vida
con larga vestidura
como monja
sin resuello
su luz
arrebatada
su corona
hecha añicos
pateada por el suelo
gente indígena nativa
quisieron ayudarla
Chicanos, Chicanas
igualmente correteados
asiáticos y negros
¿en dónde vives?
en nueva york
¿cómo te llamas?
me dicen
la estatua
de libertad

Kiss In Rift Valley
Sophia

You are the brightest of the stars in the crowd
A Kiss of gentle moss
pumping my heart
a rhythm with the grass

Your kiss divided my love,
Which is as pure as feathers of a swan
Your tenderness divided the whole starry night
Rising to stare at the universe
Only you, in the night sky pattern
Bowing to sing the Buddhist
Only you, in the song is full of you

A slight surprise
For a drought heart
A rare rain

Missing, have to be
Trapped, unable to escape already

My obsession might be Zhuang Sheng Xiao Meng
My infatuation might be the dream of Nan ke

Under the same sky
At the same cold night
The one I kissed, is peaceful as the moon
The one kissed me, is bright as the sun
Your eyes are a torch
for me eternal brilliant

Maybe for you it's just a kiss without surprise
But for me, that is,
The deepest, The deepest kiss
Deep into the East African Rift Valley, the Valley

最深一吻

你是人群里最闪亮的那一颗星
却给不及小草
青苔般的我，轻轻一吻

你的亲吻剥夺了我爱你的友情
你的柔情,割据了整个星夜
我抬头凝望,
夜空只有你，在梵唱
我低头梵唱,
歌声全是你，在凝望

一丝惊喜
给久旱的心
一场甘霖

思念，情非得已
深陷，情不自已

执迷你又恐是庄生晓梦
迷恋你又惧是南柯一梦

一样的星空下
一样的冷夜里
吻我的是独一无二的你
我吻的是皎如日月的你
你那如炬的目光,
将是我毕生的辉煌

也许那对于你而言只是轻轻一吻,不足为奇
但对于我,那就是,
最深,最深。
最深的一吻
深到东非大裂谷，谷底

Oda Al Café
Aseneth Garza

Cafecito que hace mi abuela
      Tan dulce como su sonrisa
Café amargo
      Tan fuerte que te despierta a golpes

Eres el ritual de todos los días
Seria inusual no tomarte hoy

Vienes de todas partes y te preparan de distintas maneras
Vienes de manos trabajadoras y cansadas

Llegas hacia mí y no siempre me acuerdo de tu origen
Pero tú vienes de alguien y debo recordarlo

Café dulce, café amargo
Estoy lista para este trago.

Ode To Coffee
Aseneth Garza

Coffee that my grandmother makes
    So sweet as her smile
Bitter coffee
    So strong that it wakes you up with blows

You are the ritual of my everyday life
It would be unusual to not drink you today

You come from many places and you are prepared in
diverse ways
You come from working and tired hands

You arrive to me and I don't always remember your origin
But you come from someone and I must remember that

Sweet coffee, bitter coffee
I am ready for this drink.

Bonded
Jane Wenninger

Fifty years working on oneness
Hours at the colonoscopy center
Exhausted before end of day
Bedding down early

I lie beside the body of the soul I love

Old people noises
Burps from behind
A glance beyond the ceiling
Gratitude

Even for the discordant drumbeat of Gas!

Dead End
Vincent Cooper

There was something pretty about the junkie
Walking beside . . . asking for money
Like a curiosity and a maniacal mood swing to join in and
get wired
Evading him to ride the VIA bus
He walks away towards a corner market

I see a row of dead-end streets
Staring out the window the view of broken down blue
houses
A filthy German Shepherd's tongue lying helpless on the dirt
swarmed with flies
A fifteen minute train stop, overheated cars, and a headache
setting in
Feliz Navidad signs and Christmas lights in the middle of July
The smell of old humid death
This is how I remember it
This is how it is

Covered in faded murals of significant Mexicans
Ice cream van driving by with circus happy sounds
Heat rising from the streets
As barefooted pregnant women yell at their stray children
Old ladies pushing a grocery cart collecting soda and beer
cans
Tattooed men smoking Black n' Milds, laced, and a
polarizing stare
I'd boarded the bus thankful for the cool air and brief
freedom

Choosing a Cane at Twenty-Seven
Katherine Hoerth

Everything about a medical
supply store screams *I'm dying*, from the dim
florescent lights, the dust, and to the rack,
stocked with old man canes in dreary shades
of brown. Where are the walking sticks with diamond
collars, flashy rhinestones, tipped with gold?
I want a snazzy cane that sparkles, catches
sunlight like my eyes do when I'm gazing
at the gulf at dawn. Give me a cane
in fuchsia, bright and lovely like cenizo
blooms in May, a cane that I can stroll
with, swaying hips and holding head up high
while walking through the busy downtown streets
wearing a sundress, orthopedic heels.
I want a cane that's sturdy, made for leaning
on, can bear my flesh and bones and heart,
a cane that says I'm still a human being,
whole, upright and moving through the world
at my unhurried pace, each step a triumph
of the body's will to overcome.

Slave
Müesser Yeniay

After a war
I was captured
with the chains
like my braid

I came from the North
on a horseback
for booty

on the slave market
my sealed lips
never opened

with the voice of a merchant
my body scattered into
hands of strangers

I waited for my owner
to unchain me
into a desolate dream

his eyes went down
to see me clearly
in the veil

It Was Overcast In Belfast
Eduardo R. Vega

It was overcast in Belfast
the day we took the unauthorized
black cab tour.
Cabbie took us to a slum
where the UVF held court
Murals filled the sides of apartments
remembered martyrs
inspiring successive generations
Painted walls of cemetery scenes
filled with headstones
names I recognized from newspapers
Irish leaders that weren't dead,
Yet

The other side of a wall
Republican Catholics in the same Irish poverty
as their Protestant brothers
Their own murals
remembered martyrs
inspiring successive generations
Painted walls of hatred and ignorance.

A long tall wall was built to separate them
Blockade of RPG Avenue
forcing Molotov cocktails into higher trajectories

The cabbie drove us out passed the neighborhood
desolate section of the wall
stopping as we grew nervous
handed me a permanent marker
motioned toward the wall

Maybe it's a cultural thing that I knew exactly what to do

The first and only time in my life that I've ever tagged a wall

I wrote a message of peace, signed it with our names

Today, I wonder
if she remembers that our names
are on the same side of the wall

Shelled Peas
Joyce Gullickson

Shelled peas
In cellophane bags at HEB
remind me of you
Your hands cradling the shoots
thumb and forefinger soft-shoeing
down the pod. We never danced, you and I
I stepped on your steel-toed boots
sometimes, hoping for affection
Unaware of your need for silence,
space, a cigarette

Only now, cradling cellophane packs
of purple hulls, do I feel your hands
lifting me, onto your lap
You rarely laughed, and yet
I sense contentment,
as if the rules of time and space
could somehow be lifted,
could bring us together
A scent of Old Spice,
tobacco, and carbon black
brings me back,
It's as if you lifted me again

In Bed
Viktoria Valenzuela

A tormented pile of chocolate wrappers on my bed,
Because my poet says he may not visit.
Living single means,
I dream of his voice in my ear.
The train blows its horn
a clear message to miss him all the more.
A bird chirps at dusk and I wonder if it is a toad or a locust that
has lost its best friend
to the barrio.

The train chimes again, this time more soulful sounding.
I hiccup, drunk on chocolate candy, whiskey is no longer
an option.
In my precarious condition,
I light a stick of incense.
A car drives by, the serpentine belt sounds like a wino laughing,
or a desolate woman crying alone in bed.
A dog down the street howls
Soulful like Chavela's *Paloma Negra*.

Hers is a lamenting break in sound, met with the constant peeping
of that distressed locust
or toad or bird
There are no missed messages from my poet.
My bed grows warm underneath me, I turn away.
Sleep is coaxing me to clear all thoughts.
I miss him.
Suddenly, my poet arrives to my bedside.
I blush, rising for a kiss.

He melts into my arms,
we spend the night in love.
I'd hid the chocolate wrappers
Under my pillow.
The next day lays against my face like
A wedding veil.
He asks me to marry him in bed,
A bed of our own making.

Cuando Hablo En Español
Aseneth Garza

Cuando hablo español me gusta como soy.
Soy

    Una chica enamorada con el mundo.
    Una chica con muchos sentimientos y muchos sueños.

Me siento más grande.
Y cuando estoy en Latinoamérica, me siento inmensa.

When I Speak Spanish

When I speak Spanish, I like the way that I am.
I am

    A girl enamored with the world.
    A girl with many feeling and many dreams.

I feel bigger.
And when I am in Latin America, I feel immense.

The Man In The Picture
Linda Romero

I don't remember the man
in the picture, the man I stand
like, with a hand on my hip, one
knee slightly bent

The one I repeated every swear
word to in English or Spanish
so that I would never say them again

The one who brought me surprises
after trips away – they mixed in with
gifts of "just because" or "I love you",
so now I don't know which was which

The one who bought me a ticket
to the history show at the IMAX theatre –
he looked in the Texas heat for the car
he didn't want Mom to know he lost
in the paid parking lot in San Antonio

The one who when I went to Spain gave
me a calling card for emergencies –
He went speechless when the phone
bill was more than $500 because he
"just wanted to hear [my] voice"

The one whose face I saw age almost twice
its years – cancer treatments and a brain
tumor wiped out recollections of feeding
the cats, turning on the lights in the back
and coming home.

He still gives me money every week

"to get a hamburger", and gets mad
I walk the half a block from work
because it's too hot outside

More and more I know only the man
who stands in front of me, and more
and more I forget the man in the picture.

Así Como La Lluvia
Nephtalí De León

Así como la lluvia
vino ella
    coqueta y juguetona
    fresca y risueña
    llena de amor y de alegría

Yo,
besé lo fresco de su boca
    jugué yo entre la selva de su pelo

    y ella me daba
    de noche sus estrellas
    de día el tibio calor
        de su mirada

más algo así como la lluvia de huracanes
una noche explotó entre sus ventanas
paredes y retratos

y esa lluvia
que en tiempos refrescara
los vidrios y ventanas de mi vida
    vieron chubasco y nube
    noches sin luna
    pájaros heridos

    y así como volaron
    las hojas con el viento,
    voló
    mi corazón . . .

Crash
Vincent Cooper

I spoke to a man who said he was late on his bill.
He was in a car crash a couple of months back.

He'd survived his wife.

A crack in his voice still there
Like the windshield that caught his wife's forehead
He struggled to speak her name
I could not help him.
He extended his hand to a framed picture of her and slowly
hung up on me.

A Wednesday sun dried the blood.
The EMT zipped her up.
A cleaning crew swept it up.
The commuters were late to work.

I imagined my own wife,
Dead at a steering wheel,
An unknown number on my cell phone,
A silent,, lifeless home,
Our family at the dinner table,
never speaking,
only eating her cooked leftovers
flavored with tears, hiccups, and choking back.

That night I went home and kissed her deeply,
like the first time our lips met.
My eyes crashed into her skull as our mouths collided.
My lips could not be plucked by the Jaws of Life from her.
The baby cried out from the crib,
like an ambulance siren.
My tears bled down her *canela* brown chest

like drops of blood
left by broken glass fragments and tire scraps
of someone else's wife, months ago.

We fell asleep holding hands, promises of I love you, on our
lips,
while a man sat alone,
closing his eyes,
almost hearing the last *I love you's*.

December Evening
Terry Jude Miller

remember how I held your face
in my word hungry hand

I was overcome
with the thought of loneliness

the darkness that lives in light
when it shines on someone no longer there

I was thinking of an intolerable world —
the one without you

I held your face, my eyes
brought you within me

so that death
could not take you

The Protesters Were Gone
Harold Rodinsky

leaving the streets quickly,
as the tanks showed up
with soldiers trailing behind,
feeling nervous, not invincible

in their hurry to clear the streets,
to make room for police dressed like soldiers, and soldiers
dropped placards, their demands ignored
by faceless men dressed for combat

later after the tanks and police/soldiers passed through,
orange-suited prisoners, with brooms and buckets
making 50 cents an hour
swept listlessly, barely restoring the street

the sweepers' brooms missed the ideas,
the demonstrators brought,
and left behind, in their hurry,
littering the streets, with ideas of justice

qui custodit ipsos custodes?

The Fall: Legacy Of War
Arturo Saldaña

In another time, when I was less than I now am
But more than I was before,
I flew through life with all the arrogance of youth,
Believing I had power over the world
And with words, I was capable of changing the illusion of
life.
So it was one day, I sat on the sill of a window
Pleading with another young man not to jump from the
ledge
On the seventh floor.

This is what he said:
I do not know the remedy to be given at that moment, that
second
When one understands quite well the end of dreams and
aspirations
When one's soul feels completely exhausted and says "no
more."

Someone, please, turn out the light that illuminates the
futility of my life
Close the door so I may hide in my solitude
Extinguish whatever candle that still dances in the darkness

Now, now all will is gone, no sighs, nor expectations
In truth, I prefer the night with its black blanket
That entombs me in its silence and hides the sadness of the
day
I go, without a footprint or a thumbprint,
No sighs in absolute leave I as a record of my existence
Nor a single note or word shall stay to engender a eulogy.

Someone, please, turn out the light that illuminates the

futility of my life
Close the door so I may hide in my solitude
Extinguish whatever candle that still dances in the darkness.

He stopped talking, looked at me and said "thank you."
Another glance at the glittering stars in the sky, then he
jumped.
He fell like an angel expelled from his own hell,
Dancing in the air, smoothly, slowly
Until, like all flying entities, he landed.
As the fire of his candle extinguished.

Breath of Life
José Rafael Castilleja

Gold in the sky,
Silver in your eyes.

I enter the world of mystery,
The lives of the fallen,
The lives of the living.

Good stream of stars in the sky
Guide our spirited life.

We who we are,
Few who we are,
A piece of the whole,
To make our whole and true.

Be it life or death,
We are one till the end.

In this world we call life
We are one till the end.

In this world we call life,
We are the kin of kings,
The kin of Knights,
The kin of kin.

One breath for life.

Final Prognosis
Jane Wenninger

He is dejected   Morose
Enveloped in an eerie shroud of anger

You received bad results?

The Worst

I am hampered by helplessness.
Would you like a prayer?

A shrug   A sneer   Then a grunt
Why not

I put my hand on his shoulder
I mutter a few words
Then I mutter one or two more

He begins to whimper
Jesus   Jesus   Jesus
Jesus   Oh, Jesus

Then, with wisps of strength
Jesus   Jesus   Jesus   Jesus
Oh   Oh Jesus

He sobs
Oh Jesus   Jesus   Oh Jesus
. . . Jesus?

His face shimmers.
Sweet Jesus   Oh   my sweet, sweet Jesus
Yes sweet Jesus   Yes   Yes   Yes

We are silenced   Softened

He removes my hand from his shoulder

He kisses my fingers
He looks me full in the face

And says, Thank you.

Thank you for reminding me of
Who I know

Ishmael and Isaac
Oscar C. Peña

The halls of warriors are hallowed
By the words of those who grieve.

A Father's Lament

Old eyes carved deep in leathered skin
Passed down from Father Abraham.
Mohammed el Hasim rasps — *Welcome! Sit! Eat!*
He shares his meal of fire roasted chicken
In its black skin, and there's a great fried fish
Tail curled in hot oil agony
Served with roasted red and yellow peppers
On a platter of rice with almonds
And pistachios.

Six thousand miles away in Mississippi
An old man sits down to picnic on the grounds
Of the Jackson Primitive Baptist Church.
Sunday lunch is mashed potatoes and black-eyed peas
Fried chicken and collard greens, pitchers of iced sweet tea.
There are four kinds of cake —
White, chocolate, carrot and strawberry.
Preacher says the blessing

Mohammed el Hasim watches his son walk out the door.
Another man's American boy, no child of innocence
Though raised in the Bethel Church, but learned
And trained, he is a man who looks to war
Because he can.
Dust and smoke plumes rise in Baghdad streets
Emptied except for shadows.
Both sons don their battle gear.
Their enemies they will kill.

Their fathers pray to God.

I Want To Exalt Your Laughter In This Language
Julieta Corpus

You walked in like the light
Dancing with blue-green waves
In the Atlantic Ocean
Shimmering hypnotically
I fell silent—no I must've retorted
Something clever when you spoke
To me about the heat
Your laughter intimated passion
Interlaced with youthful gaiety
Your laughter exposed my world
Revealing a crushing nothingness
Strangling this sad man
Your laughter aroused all senses
Unleashing a torrent
I could not restrain
The unbridled joy in your laughter
Placated ardent sorrows
Your laughter silenced doubt.

My 30 Cats And I
Ann Fogelman

scale a narrow ledge
we sit
and watch
the world go by

to entertain
themselves
my cats

stare
leer
grin coquettishly

sit quietly
prance
dance with two left feet
front and back that is

they miaow miaow
loudly
threaten
tease

one cat nibbles her paw
she stepped on a pancake
coated with syrup

the world passing by
stops
to watch
my 30 cats and me

My Brown Is On The Inside
Eloísa Pérez-Lozano

Though my skin is fair
My brown is on the inside
Waiting to be revealed

Inside the pages of Anaya, Cisneros, Álvarez
The sustenance of my soul
Inside the tenderness of my eyes
Shining at a baby's giggle

Inside my ears filled with joy
As Mexico scores
The commentator's jubilant cry
Going on and on and on

Inside the *chiles serranos*[1] and *cebolla picada*[2]
The edges frying to a golden honey
The spice tickling my nose and throat
Teasing my taste buds

Inside my hands, my visual voices
Weaving and slicing through the air
Feelings through animated fingers
Setting volleyballs and writing out worlds

Inside the curve and sway of my hips
Swirling and swerving to the sounds of salsa
Provoking passionate, playful pivoting
My toes digging down into the floor

Inside the maroon chambers of my heart
Where *La Virgencita*[3] bounces to its beat
Inside the Spanish I speak
Tan natural como respirar[4]

Inside my papá's long, lanky arms
Embraces, gentle and soothing
His bellowing laugh
Echoing my own

Inside my mamá's *"mijita linda"*[5]
Expresiones de cariño[6] encircling me
Inside her endless spoiling
No matter how old I am or will be

[1] Serrano peppers
[2] Diced onion
[3] The Virgin of Guadalupe
[4] As natural as breathing
[5] My sweet daughter
[6] Expressions of endearment

Creación
Mateo Mansilla Moya

Nacimos para crear.
En nuestros trazos
buscamos la perfección
que anhelamos.

En las letras graficamos
la complejidad
de nuestras ideas,
y las usamos para formar palabras.

Con las palabras
describimos nuestros sentimientos,
y plasmamos en papel
nuestros pensamientos.

Todo lo conectamos
creando sistemas
para transmitir a los demás
nuestros conocimientos.

Creamos historias posicionándonos
en situaciones diferentes.
Creamos ritmos
intentando ser coherentes.

Creamos. Sí, creamos.
Creamos por egoísmo.
Creamos por la necesidad
de satisfacernos a nosotros mismos.
Creamos por el placer de hacerlo.

Creamos dejando atrás
penas e incertidumbres.
Creamos porque así
nos lo proponemos.

A La Llorona
Seres J. Magana

Se escucha al anochecer su llanto en las calles
Llorando por sus hijos robados de su lecho
Sus hijos que perdidos ya la han olvidado

Que vagan igual que ella en un mundo atado
Desnudos y alimentándose del desecho
¿Pero si nadie se atreve a oír, que da cuanto chille?

Lágrimas de sangre corren bajo sus mejillas
Lágrimas de sangre sobre mi tierra morena

Country Dancing
Chip Dameron

Outside Xian, inside a renovated
farmers' village, where most men

must work the week in the city,
wives fix dinner and after dark

follow the bright streetlights
to the local schoolyard, assemble

on the back basketball court,
and do Chinese line dances,

gracefully stepping and swaying,
taped music filling the night

and quarter turning them again,
culminating in "Cotton-Eyed Joe,"

as if they were booted Texans,
waiting for the rodeo to start.

Perseverant Possums
Kathy Trenfield Raines

In high-pitched panting zeal,
Yellow lab bounds upward, squealing,
Jaws snapping at possum's stolid, resolute feet.
Possum methodically traces the fence top,
One clawed foot in front of the other,
Not deigning to dive into safe backyard.
Nonplussed possum continues his trek.

I've tried to beat a possum off the fence with a stick, into
asylum;
Wobbling a bit, he stayed true to his chosen path.
Possums persevere.

While possum sits on low limb,
Foolish dogs, passions afire, hurl themselves inches away;
Possum growls, scolds, but stays till dog is spent.

If indeed captured, possum transforms self to seeming
death,
Frozen, malodorous as a dead rat
Till silly dog loses interest.
And possum trods away.

If he is gored, if he is killed, so be it.
Like that extra set of teeth in a shark's gums,
Another comrade takes his place.

Rose Bud, (ADHD)
Richard Sánchez

Attention Deficit, Hyperactive Disorder
You're messing with my mind
It's too much; I can't keep up.
When I'm asleep, supposedly resting
My brain is alive and my body is jerking
Random movements, kicking spasms
My mind is on fire,
A pot of boiling water
A rolling boil, poor lobster in a pot
a symphony on warm ups
A chaotic sea of instruments
Synapses firing practice notes
All systems go, no start,
just full speed ahead, No finish
"on a road that leads to nowhere"
If I could only be normal, like you,
calm, and without sedation
If I could just be mellow, ordinary
Turn my brain down to simmer
Maybe one day I'll be okay,
I'll take the scenic route,
Take the country side road,
Stop for coffee . . . smell the roses
before they wilt, before the petals fall . . .

The Songs We Sang
James Griswold

Before me was the face of stage IV terminal cancer.
No chemo or radiation would be given.
No hope, no future was offered,
except which flowed through the plastic tubes
into his swollen veins to control his pain.
His eyes dull and lifeless,
reflected the destruction of body and spirit
that this insidious disease had taken on my brother,
once so vibrant and alive.

I didn't know what to do or say, so I sang for him.
Actually, I sang as much for myself as for him.
I sang the soulful chants that we shared a love for,
that we learned in the cathedral we grew up in;
Gregorian chants and hymns to our merciful God.
I stroked his shoulder and held his hand
and sang "Lord have mercy, Christ have mercy,"
wiping the tears away as I realized
that the mercy I was praying for was his speedy passing.

I longed for the days when his deep baritone
would meet my tenor as we tried to outdo each other;
"How great Thou art, How great Thou art!"
So I sang it solo. His eyes met mine with a flicker of
memory.
In that moment, I felt an eerie feeling of joy.
We shared that last song, though he sang only with his eyes.
He squeezed my hand and we were in the cathedral once
again.
The ancient organ bellowed shaking the air mightily.
Our voices resonated and filled the cathedral with glory!
"So sing my Soul my savior God to thee…."
Always will I cherish our final song.

Coffee Cups 3
Jeannette Moreno McNeill

Problems need fixing?
In the dishing business, coffee cups
are certified ceramic
good-time tools . . .

Modified ovenware, stoneware,
microwave-proof, and even glass,
the makings of
good-time cups..

Inscriptions, instantly
bring back
the town,
the city,
the person,
and suddenly, you're not alone.
Floating in images,
you're at home.

Coffee does that to you.
You come home to yourself
in a thousand ways.

Coffee cups are being replaced
with Thermos bottles,
safely put in drive-to-work cars
snuggled inside round cubby holes.

Disposable carry-out cups
with cardboard handles and too-hot
coffee is hurried along . . .

The coming home to yourself
is being replaced
by a lost, lonely feeling of panic.

And the problems?
They're not getting fixed.

The Sky Speaks To Us In San Antonio
Viktoria Valenzuela

When the sky is purple and starlit, it is night
and time to hold close the one I love.

When the sky cries fat tears for the cacti, it is daytime
and time to hold back pain like thorns.

When sky says all the words ever spoken, it is January
and I know there is poetry in the wind sweeping from our
lips to our hair.

Leaves, Autumn
Homer Starkey

We fall, are grieved, decay
Like the sins we bring,
Our imperfections,
Our championed things

Now the world of lofty song —
These bucolic gardens —
Fossilize in disrepair;
The heart and phloem hardens

Our punishment is this:
Not limbo or hell or black,
But days finding ways to make more days,
None of which exact

Maybe We Were Children
Weasel

When the leaves stole our
imagination in the Autumn,
and the river turned into
 a street corner full of
cities in its cracks, the
jazzman's solemn trumpet
graces the footsteps of
our past as we swam
into rising waters. Someone
called out for us, we heard
them, but our ears never
picked up on their
voice. Maybe we were
children, sitting in the
cool Autumn river, our
past just floating around
us. But we are ghosts,
and ghosts never carry a past.

Coyote
Beto Conde

He stopped on the far side of the street and looked back.
Our eyes met for a shattered second.
I sensed a connection
I saw survival
In my mind, in those wild yellow eyes flashing by,
I saw his soul
I thought I saw my soul,

A coyote dashed across the road in front of me.
already at full speed before stepping on the road,
he streaked across my eyes.
Running from something someone before turning his gaze at
me
before our vision collided and connected
our eyes met, his panicked, mine amazed.

Coyote with your eyes on fire,
surviving overwhelming odds against you
Surviving among not so kind human kind
I saw the panic, the courage, the strength in eyes flashing.
forever on the alert, always ready to run for your life,
literally.

I sensed the panic, the courage, the confidence in your eyes
flashing at mine.
I stopped in my tracks to admire you,
How can I relate my respect and admiration?
Impossible but to my mind
I wanted to share, I know where you are.
The fear, the courage, the strength to survive the odds

I salute you, Coyote on the run
I admire you, Coyote on hyper vigilance

Flashing across my eyes
Sometimes I am you

In the sometimes monotonous routine everydays of life
Sometimes we forget we are alive
some days, some simple incident just awakes the world
again

Un coyote con ojos de sol
Corriendo a todo vuelo cruzó mi paso
habló conmigo

I saw the Coyote say, I'm alive,
I heard the Coyote say, you're alive!

From McAllen to Austin Metronormativity
Charles McGregor

Some queers need to leave home in order to become queer, and others need to stay close to home in order to preserve their difference.
– Judith Halberstam, *In a Queer Time & Place*

Small town boy with a degree, small town boy that wants to leave
wears busy skinny jeans, a headband colored with hippie spittle.
He asks the assumption: *So, when you headed to Austin?*
Praise be to cosmo queer paradise, an ivory tower blessing
for the suburban gay boy that won't imagine cul-de-sac transformations.

I think Austin boys — they rub my furry fingers, talk bars
and Bronze Age bathhouses and lament suburban martyrdom —
the hetero scene we're plagued to navigate. There's the McAllen gay bar
safely off of the 17th St. strip. McAllen boys think old men —
bunker queers watching midnight drag hump the floor, bite the air.

The small town boy talks of the mentality of ghetto queer bars
facing off against cis suburbia. He will head to Austin,
student loans subsidizing in his tiny back pocket,
looking for that like-minded spirit. Queer studies knows branding —
the escape of white flight suburbia in this Chican@ town —

the urbane paradise of Austin. The cloth expressing identity,
the bars wasting boys that leave a nest that needs fixing,
needs the local queer to negotiate the new suburbia.

Temptation
Ashley Hodgson

I keep waiting for old age —
for the aggregate of my regrets —
to outweigh the pulling fullness of my lust.
I wait for the comfort of routine
to overshadow the glistening globe of honey
oozing from the hive.
The golden glow of that earthly sweetness appears slowly,
ferments in a drop,
and lingers for a long time,
hanging by a thin, sticky line.

How the Body Heals
Katherine Hoerth

What else could you do but begin your grieving,
weep for all the branches the storm had snapped in
two, the oak tree dripping with loss, the windblown
fence that was leaning

to the sodden soil, lantanas lying
supine underneath all the weight of water
drowning like you drown every day in your pain. But
this is how healing

comes – it simply happens. Let crows devour
what no longer lives, the disease. Let fire
ants march off with pieces of petals. Let the
roots find their strength to

try again, to snake through the ground like nerves through
skin, through flesh, through bone. Let them swallow
rain, let pain evaporate like a puddle in the
sunshine, a droplet

at a time. Let vines overcome the fallen
fence, unfurl their leaves like new skin, their flowers
flush with life and pollen. Let nature take its
course. Let the wind wash

off the scent of dying. Let bones reset, muscles
flourish, strength return like the hummingbirds in
autumn. Let it happen again, your body
thrumming with healing.

Viejito With A Cane
Eduardo R. Vega

I stood in line
behind
un viejito with a cane
buying pan dulce
and candles of el sagrado corazón.

A dozen panecillos
six veladoras
one timid cashier
wondering
how he's going to prevent
Jesus' sacred heart
from breaking.

I Tried
Lamar Jones

Maaaan how you gone come at me with that one last kiss
proposition
when I was exhausting all my options
you paid me no nevermind
when all I wanted was a chance
Now it seems convenient for you and all of a sudden you
tryin'
to put another monkey wrench in the plans
See there you go wit' that emotional rollercoaster you had
me ridin on
when in the beginnin' you seemed down and ready for the
ride-along
Until things got rough and them marriage edges got refined
and rigid
Funny how regret settles in
Funny how finding out that the grass ain't always green will
bring you back to earth at meteor speed
Bring you back to reality and I ain't talkin' 'bout tv
These feelings are undeniably real
At first there was a shame associated with the questions
And I was full of self doubt— no question
But I'm good now
I vicariously awaited for the day that you would come
around
Who knew that the delegated decibels of silence could sound
off so loud
But it gave me time to think
Gave me time to figure if I was gone swim or if I was gone
give in
to those ankle weights shackled to my flesh and sink
Life has new meaning
And I refuse to live life on a whim
As I gaze out into the turbulent waters

My mind is made up
I can't stop now
I have no choice
Lives depend on me making it
My only option at this point is to mentally prepare for a
soul-cleansing,
Life-altering journey of a swim
So I press on

Ultimo Poema
JoAnn DeLuna

Que se sepa:
trate, falle, ame, llore, conquiste
y nunca estuve satisfecha,
hasta que supieras que siempre pensaba en ti —
siempre fuiste mi motivación y inspiración.
Para enseñarte que, tú también eras poeta.
Para que entiendas que, tú también podías entender
sujetos complicados y emociones tan profundas.
Para que sepas que, tu vida fue poesía.
Cada plato que lavaste,
cada baño que limpiaste,
cada gota de sudor que derramaste
y lagrima que lloraste,
cada dolor y angustia que cargaste
para sobre vivir un nuevo día,
cada uña que sacrificaste y cada dedo que sangraste
fueron poemas escritos en tu sangre,
testimonios de amor.
Cada vez que no pudiste comunicar con tu jefe,
cada malentendido con la gente
fueron exploraciones en dicción.
Cada vez que estuviste muy cansada
pero te levantaste para un nuevo amanecer.
El momento cuando decidiste huir de tu país,
de lo conocido a lo desconocido,
con la fe que tus hijos pudrieran vivir
una vida mejor,
una vida sin hambre,
una vida sin sed,
una vida libre y llena de amor.
Para que entiendas que,
tú fuiste la voz de millones,
como tú, quienes no encontraron las palabras para hablar.
Para que sientas que
tus hijos fueron tus mejores poemas.

Last Poem
JoAnn DeLuna

Let it be known:
I tried, I failed, I loved, I cried, I conquered
And was never satisfied
Until you'd recognize, you were always on my mind.
You always were my motivation.
So you'd fathom,
You, too, were a poet.
So you'd realize,
You, too, could understand complicated subjects
And profound emotions.
So you'd acknowledge
Your life was poetry.
Every dish washed
Every bathroom cleaned,
Every drop of sweat shed
Every tear spilled
Every pain and anguish carried to survive a new day,
Every sacrificed fingernail
And every finger bled
Was a poem written in your blood,
Testimonies of love.
Every failed attempt to communicate with your boss
And each moment lost in translation,
Were explorations in diction.
Every exhausting morning you'd still rise to face another day,
The instant you decided to leave your country, from the known to
the unknown,
With only the faith your kids would be able to live a better life,
A life without hunger,
A life without thirst,
A life of freedom and full of love.
So you'd accept,
You were the voice of millions just like you,
Who could not find the words to speak.
So you'd feel
Your kids were your greatest poems.

The Scream
After Viewing Edvard Munch's
Der Schrei Der Natur (The Scream Of Nature)
Loretta Diane Walker

If you let go of your Halloween
peanut-candy corn-coated breath,
it will become a ghost in the city of Odessa.
Not like that cheery chubby Casper cartoon
or those grotesque movie ghouls.
Rather a spirit of relief floating in an October chill.
Is this how we make the world small?
Through breath and air?
Maybe the redwoods in California
will smell the sweet aroma of your release.

If you dress yourself in a coat of curiosity
while driving around these overcrowded concrete streets,
you will see the city's dress is summer green
with a hem of frightened yellow, drab brown
and a collar of panicked orange.
Munch mimics fall with the same hues
in *Der Schrei der Natur.*
This contorted face he sketched
in his whirlwind of colors
is no more terrifying than my dreams
rummaging through the darkness, fishing for stars.
Is this what fear looks like,
a distorted jaw and murky shadows?
If so, does a violet scream joy?

If we wait until tomorrow to remove our masks,
truth will follow us into November.
You will see beneath this flesh I am a pole.
Your words lean against everything you once feared.

Scales
After Wallace Stevens
Laura Peña

The night is a serpent
slithering over the breakwaters.

It slinks over undulating sands
and between your feet.

It spreads its shroud everywhere —
its engulfing shroud.

The cerecloth fastens to your body
and is transformed

by the skin and teeth of you.
The filaments of your eyes

tear on the edges of the breakwaters
and in the grains of the shifting sands.

Reading Up on Ecuador
PW Covington

Pilgrims still seek these shores
But, I'm reading up on Ecuador
With a dog and a cat at my feet
Out on my Texas porch

It's a sunny, winter, day
Like the houseplants,
I've pulled myself outside for sun
Waiting for Kerouac to amble up my street

We'll swap stories about
Ships and Disability benefits,
VA hospitals and riding in stolen cars
We will not speak of poetry
And I will not share my wine

I'm reading up on Ecuador
They say it's easy living
in a land that isn't yours
Freed from all responsibility

To fix, to clean up, to plant, to teach
No need to sweat, or serve, or toil, or bleed
The expatriate life;
Behind doors, Behind walls, Behind gates
Down streets with signs printed in English
Antiseptic isolation
A life of Yankee leisure
What would Wm. Burroughs do?
The Rio Grande Valley still looks great
This time of year
Palm Trees, Palm Trees
10th street in McAllen

It runs on, and on, and on

God bless them, God bless them
With the Beatest prayer I ever learned

As it was in the beginning, Is now, And ever will be

I'm reading up on Ecuador

Beard Meditation
César Leonardo De León

I want to let my beard grow
Down to my chest
To cover my scars.

Down to my groin
To hide the Devil and God.

Down to my scraped knees,
My tired feet.

I want it to grow out the door
In the middle of the night
Into neighborhoods,

Topple political signs growing
In gardens instead of flowers.

I want it to climb up
Radio and TV towers,
Provide silence for a change.

I want it to go into libraries,
Get tangled in pages,
Snagged in commas, question marks,
Long sentences with semicolons.

I want it to wind down
Old country roads and get dusty.

Into woods through paths
No longer trodden.

Along forgotten coastlines

Southward to the pole.

Let it spill out into space.
Until it finds a resting place
Along the edge of the galaxy.

Let it grow an eye and an ear
Before I pull it back
One inch at a time.

Shadow Of A Dream
LuLynne Streeter

The highway to Chihuahua
Rises from the floor of the Valley,
Past the restaurant La Cuesta.

Roses and bougainvillea
Shade the verandah.
Grackles cry in the canopy.

Tangled grapevines twine
Against blue plaster walls.
White linen cloths flutter.

To the west, the setting sun
Burns the mountains black.
An old woman pats tortillas.

Piquant scents rouse
Appetites and conversation.
Colored lights sway in breeze.

Sonoran brandy warms the blood.
A waning moon illuminates
Our farewell caress.

Almost Forgotten
Terry Jude Miller

the bluebird in the holly tree
takes flight and the rest of the afternoon
follows him

the branch where he perched
waves goodbye, oscillating
in scarlet fractions to stillness

now I wonder if he was ever there
or is he conjured from memories
of a boy in his brother's hand-me-down coat
walking the edge of the woods
that held the family farm in place

perhaps also the boy has taken
to the air of never returning

a tattered map in his mouth
muffles his bird song

Beltane
Walter Birdwell

The Wise Woman and the Sage
Sit back a ways from the fire
Lit every year on Beltane Eve
They slowly kissed and reminisced.

They listen to the songs and drums
Watch the youths and maidens dance
It does not seem that very long ago
They were the King and Queen of May.

Young men and women leap the flames
They drink deep of cups of golden mead
Pairing off and disappearing into the forest
Partaking of their more private celebrations.

The smoke from the Beltane fire
Forms figures in the moving wisps
Figures rising to the starry sky
Out of the fiery elemental heat.

The Great Goddess and Horned God above
Look down and bless the happy ceremony
They smile on the old embracing couple.
They bestow a special blessing on them.

Anything Welcome
(on the way to Hippie Hollow)
Trevor Wainwright

Homeless, life a mess
His sign said "Anything welcome, God bless"
I gave him some change from my pocket
"Thank you, Sir," he said,
So why instead of feeling good
Did I look away and cry instead?

Tierra Caliente,
TepalcaTépec, Michoacán (Jan. 22, 2014)
Nephtalí De León

mira mi pueblo querido
mira lo que ha sucedido
allá por TepalcaTépec
estado de Michoacán . . .

sin fiestas ni quinceañeras
nadie salía por las calles
demonios hacián pedazos
pueblo corazón del pueblo

¿qué dice la radio compa?
¿vecino dime qué dice?
ruedan las llantas del diablo
van armados los señores . . .

si morimos amarrados
dijo la gente del pueblo
sin libertad no se vive
prefiero morir de pie

del indio corrió la voz
hizo su sangre el llamado
pueblo corazón del pueblo
el pueblo se encuentra armado

antiguos guerreros tigres
con un águila en el alma
y una virgencita santa
¡ andan por Tierra Caliente !

vuela palomita vuela
las flores del camposanto
tiemblan al oír las balas
la gente limpia su pueblo
¡urgente dicen urgente!
¡lo que no hizo el presidente!

Sister Moon
Richard Sánchez

Silent, seeing, always knowing
Creeping, rising, evening falling
Full moon magic stirring bones
Silver, pewter, colored tones
Silver sister, sounding rays
Sweeping shadows from his face
Oh that I could reach in there
Toss his sandy feathered hair
What then, I beg, becomes my fate?
From dusk to dawn my heart does ache
Both death and sleep from me escape
And misty dreams are taking shape
Pillow talk no comfort brings
Sobbing sister, crying dreams
Eyes that see no angel's face,
Love is finding empty space
Yearning, patience, endless crime
Homeless gypsy sands of time
Luna, sister, speak to me
Tell me moon, what do you see?

Observations On The Whole
Mike Gullickson

"Gemini is visible tonight," someone says.
I can smell an inferior red wine
on his breath, smell scallops and linguini
see the evidence of poor fork manipulation
in a quarter sized stain
on his shirt pocket,
note his shoes have never been shined---
so I know where he lives,
how he lives,
and where he dined.

But I can't see the constellations,
I never could
I can only see the stars
and that's enough for me.

All God's Creatures
(Austin Wildlife Rescue)
Trevor Wainwright

One of my tour's features is helpin' the smaller of God's
creatures
My choice cos' it's said he hears even the smallest voice
Little bird, baby possum or rabbit,
Creatures of the night, creatures of habit
Winged, four-footed large or small I'll be there to help 'em
all

The Ragged Landscape
Richard Sánchez

Across the ragged landscape
I witnessed a parade
The multitudes cheered loudly
Some cried for an escape
At dusk the crowd did linger
Dark clouds with scattered rain
White lightening split the darkness
The earth did feel His pain
Anguished heart exhausted
Dark eyes no longer see
But scarlet splattered droplets
Crossed beams, a set of three
Beyond the purple mountains
On a hill once made of stone
The weeping crowd, released Him
And my heart was not alone
From right to left a vision
Low laid His Bleeding Crown
Stained red the purple garments
The King of Kings was found

Pinche Damocles
Oscar C. Peña

*There can be nothing happy for the person
over whom some fear always looms.*

Cicero

He was at the Turning Basin this morning
Down on the Houston Ship Channel
Looking for work in the refineries —
Scaffolding, hydro-blasting, day labor.

No one's hiring today
Turn-around season's almost over
Things are slow, the lady said, *come by*
In a couple days.

Sitting at a table in La India Bonita
Drinking beer and eating the lunch special —
Three tacos and a bowl of you-serve-yourself beans
Pearl beer sign hangs overhead, neon gas long-gone.

Elvira's cardboard cutout stands in a corner
Her *Mistress of the Dark* cleavage selling something
Long forgotten. *El Mariachi* flickers black & white
Muted silent on TV.

Antonio Banderas pulls pistols from under his guitar
Goes to shooting. Bad men's black blood spews
Across the screen. Nobody's watching. Nobody cares.
Everything gathers dust.

The old man orders another beer
Decides he'll go back to the Turning Basin
Find some honest work.
It's better than killing himself.

Haiku 111
(El Sal Del Rey, Rio Grande Valley — Texas)
Trevor Wainwright

Salt coated, crystallized
Mummified, petrified
Like a time capsule

Hover
Lisa Adam

Some people remember flying from another incarnation, or dream about flying, or learn to fly. As a child I repeatedly dreamt about hovering, sort of floating, slowly but in the air not water, and not so languidly or splashily but rather moving calmly with my feet off the ground through the familiar aerial territory of house and yard, around unmindful family members like legs of furniture. And I chalk up a lot to these hovering dreams, in retrospect. Perhaps if I had dreamt of flying I would have traveled the world by now, I would have become a globe-trotting, book-signing novelist or activist, I would have become a creator of high-end fashion / permacultured suburbs / kinetic urban sculpture; or I would have had the courage to give up or never acquire this boatload of weighty paraphernalia that my insurance agent lists as "residence" and "household goods," and I might have learned raptor rehabilitation instead of adopting two bellicose housecats and two addled lapdogs. I would have done something where my life was not circumscribed by trips to work, supercenter, pharmacy, thrift shop, and municipal parks with their grounds littered by Popsicle wrappers and dog droppings. Perhaps I should just be glad I didn't dream about crawling, but crawling would at least mean good visceral contact, nose to the ground, fingers gripping and tracing the textures of moss, oriental carpets, prairie grass, decomposed granite, schoolroom linoleum.

But no, I just hovered.

Hovering is no-man's land. Hovering is transition. Don't people say they hover over their bodies before they "move to the light," or zoom back into corporeal life? If that's the case, at least hovering gives a little perspective--not too much distance to make things lose their resolution or too little distance to distort things with fisheye proximity, but just enough to stand back a little, hover just a bit away, to weigh, sort, discern, observe. Perhaps hovering is, after all, for poets.

Unspoken Peek-A-Boo
Jeannette Moreno McNeill

Like children's peek-a-boo,
our caring
lives hidden from view,
in the world of
silence
and exchanged glances.

Absurd,
outrageous, and yet,
sure, soft, and gentle.

Like an unwanted child,
precarious,
and fragile
in its existence.

Yet, upon its arrival,
so loved.

Challenging time
Challenging distance
Challenging even
you and me

Meteor
Sophia

 The moment match polish
Light burning eyes
Dimming vision
Warming heart

A meteor across the heart
Cut into painful
Bleeding roses
Wetting eyes

Make a vow to those stars
who are as belle as eyes
for giving me the starry eyes
Because the starry eyes
Never cry

Separated during the vast sea
Licking tears
Searching for your shadow

What a luxury to me!
Wish of memories flashing
If you're just A B C D
who I passed by

Why being a Meteor?
Why cutting my heart?

Mon Amant, in a Van Gogh painting.
Is the Egyptian mummy
Mon Amant, in a galaxy far far away
Is a transient meteor

流星

火柴刹那擦亮
灼烧眼睛的光芒
模糊视力
暖了心

流星划过心脏
割得生疼
红了玫瑰
湿了眼

向眼睛般的星辰许愿
赐予我星辰般的眼睛
因为星辰般的眼睛
不会流泪

茫茫人海
走散了
舔着泪
苦苦找寻你的身影

多么多么奢望
奢望自己薄情寡义
倘若你只是
与我擦肩而过的
甲乙丙丁

为何你却是流星？
为何擅长割我心？

Mon amant，在梵高的画里
是埃及的木乃伊
Mon amant，在遥远的星系
是稍纵即逝的流星

Psalm for Hands and Shoes
Shirley Rickett

Praise for old shoes
to pull on mornings like a life
to wear to work
to stretch a paycheck
to walk a picket line
to polish and wear again
to dance in Saturday night
to run for help
to wait in vigil
to shuffle at a wake

Praise for his hands
that took cinders
and dirt and sand
from my knee
that lifted me
from a dead faint
for her hands on my chest
for her shoes in the snow
when death
nearly took me and

Praise for the gift
of calm for when
my own came
with a fractured arm
broken skull
bleeding face
from a bad fall
when the oldest came
with the news *I'm leaving, Mom*
All praise for hands and shoes

Canadian Lake Recipe
Chip Dameron

Mix tons of rock flour
with icy snowmelt

bake under summer sun
for thousands of years

until emerald or turquoise:
serves multitudes.

A Saudi's Silk (Azhar)
Eloísa Pérez-Lozano

Before today, her English was a faltering faucet
Leaking with necessary nouns and verbs
Dripping enough to get chores done
To get through the academic day
Her voice a kind, hesitant whisper in the wind

Now, she reads in her own tongue
And the waves of Arabic gush forth
Unbridled, unburdened, and free
A waterfall, liberated from
A dam of English rules

An unseen confidence shines through
Her voice, awakened and renewed
Like the strands of a spider's silk
Weaving intricate arabesque designs
At once tough and delicate,
beautifully birthing
this Middle-Eastern masterpiece

Words I've never heard
Sounds I've never made
But they still move me,
Hold me in the valleys of their vowels
Inside their consonant cavern walls
Make me feel at home
In a foreign land
As they pour from her mouth

Holy, sacred words dancing through the air
Overflowing
Blessings to my ears.

And I Wonder . . . Simon (21)
Annika Blanke

Simon. I never knew if you were running away from a threat or running towards a goal. But I know it always depends on the pace of those around you if you can call a pathetic attempt of running a preparation for a marathon or an afternoon walk in the park. But you were never a Husain Bolt to me; you were more like a Harry Belafonte. Though you never managed to teach the world to play according to your notes, you preferred to play the world by ear anyways. "When life gives you lemons, make some lemonade." That phrase was far too boring for you, because, in fact, life gave you so many lemons you could have easily made millions by selling thousands of ice cold drinks in your front yard but instead of selling lemonade, you decided to sell your soul instead.

So when life finally handed you something steady and worthwhile in this world constantly full of changes, you grabbed it with both hands, even though it was a brand-new haircut, an Oath of Enlistment and a gun. And now I don't know where else to run. All I know is that I do not care if I'm walking or running because all I see reminds me of you and I wonder . . . how many more families in the world share the same history?! And I wonder . . . how the next generation must feel when their little son has to spell the word "freedom" in his first spelling bee when we all know this word does not actually exist! And I wonder . . . if I will ever come to terms with the fact that it was your name in the newspaper that I saw: Simon (21). You semi-fast wannabe Husain Bolt. You scratched dance instructor from Detroit, Michigan. You out-of-tune Harry Belafonte. I hope they don't hand you lemons where you are now but feed you lemonade instead. And finally call your pathetic attempt of running a full-blown marathon.

Cat God
Kathy Trenfield Raines

If God is indeed a cat,
In heaven,
We will stare at air, alert for changes.
We will creep up on swift lizards, hacking off tails,
Then attack them, still a-waggle.
We will slash and sink teeth into necks of fledgling birds,
Their mamas screaming, scolding, helpless.
Toms will capture, bite and subdue yowling queens
They won in conquest.
We will caress and be caressed
We will sleep and dream and wake and dream
We will keep excruciatingly clean,
To lovingly washed nails.
And wash our friends' faces, too.
We will watch and watch, wary always
We will know our rank, clearly,
We will play with balls and string and sticks.
We will be happy cats then,
If, in life, we adored our wise companions.

Chingón
Meliton Hinojosa, Jr.

Soy Chingón, soy bien, Chingón
I slap her,
En frente de el niño,
So he, can learn

Soy bien Chingón,
I slap my daughters around
En frente de el niño,
So he, can learn

Soy bien Chingón,
I spend all of my money,
Con mis amigos,
I buy the booze, la mota y las rucas

Soy bien Chingón,
The utilities are shut off
So, le doy chingazos a la vieja,
Even though, she is much younger

Soy bien Chingón,
Got fired from my job,
Y se vencio la renta,
And I am broke,

Soy bien Chingón,
So she'll pack the shit,
Y nos vamos a media noche,
So the landlord, won't see us

Soy bien Chingón,
Went before a female judge,
And the damn bitch
Me quito, lo Chingón

Winston
Ashley Hodgson

Whiskered beast in black
Stalking lizards in the grass
Napping on the roof

With Care and Touch of Wings
Joanne Uppendahl

Ask the bees, for they have not forgotten how to love.
Within or without the hive, their wingspans involve
the whole of each, reaching deeply into what we do

not see. They ride the current of the fractal arch
of countless rooms. With care and touch of wings,
dance rhythms click to consciousness of distance.

No teeth will bite into their span of time, for they
have not forgotten how to love; their honey glaze
feeds both larvae and our sweet-longing tongues.

At The Kitchen Table
Mike Gullickson

We talk poetry and poets
mourn the loss of Mark Strand
and Galway Kinnel.
When e.e. cummings died
I lit a small candle
that still burns.

I look at the reflections
in our new thermal coffee pot,
a fun house mirror that stretches color
stretches my hand and pen
as I write they become something else
elongated flesh a writing instrument
somehow mystical
somehow channeling another realm.
I guess it's always been that way.

We talk poetry and listen to each other,
a miracle of communication without Wi-Fi
or ISPs or anything more than the electricity
of our selves.
I ask nothing more than every day
begins like this.

Shadows
Ann Fogelman

 my mind swims
with visions
    shadows of trees
     on a pavement
and memories
     a little girl skipping
     between the light and dark
     on her way to school

Beer Goddess of the Rio Grande Valley
A Sonnet in Blank Verse
Katherine Hoerth

Who would guessed a goddess could be found
behind a bar, beneath an autumn moon,
in this oasis on the edge of town?
She crosses frothing oceans with a leap
of faith. She molds an old world out of Texas
dust. She traces rivers with her fingers,
then pours her blessings out in streams of gold
in Dunkels, heffeweissens, pilsners, blondes.

We, the thirsty come to drink it in –
her laughter and her warmth, her German charm.
We leave with bellies full, our hearts content,
our words a little slurred. Ursula,
beer goddess of the Rio Grande Valley,
thank you for your hospitality.

Overwhelmed
Joyce Gullickson

Whoever said that love can atrophy
has never been inoculated by a mist
never seen the ordinary beauty
of a falling leaf, or watched the way
a goldfinch's feathers change like sunrise

Whoever said "You can trust in this"
must have been under the influence
of nature's hallucinogens — the way air holds
a hummingbird hovering above your palm,
the healing power of touch, as your hand
reaches out, overwhelmed

The way tenderness goes on and on
forever and ever, like this

El Chubasco de Tabasco
Kjell Nykvist

Intrepid travelers who explore Tabasco feel like spun gold
Porque belleza brilla allí, incluso por la noche,
And because there's a magic to the state most visitors
behold,
Una bella magia sentída, pero que no se ve.

Tabasco is a mélange of bright, tropical colors. It is
La tierra de los flamboyanes y los guayacanes.
But also a place pounded by the wind and rain. And so it is
La tierra de vientos fuertes y lagos grandes.

Above the lush landscape, the weather swiftly makes itself
anew:
Las nubes blancas se convierten en montañas negras;
The sun vanishes; the long, sinuous rivers flow as if through
Un reino iluminado por las estrellas negras.

The travelers feel Tabasco, this land crowned with skies of
dark water:
El trueno es como un tambor; las lluvias conquistan;
Large ponds erupt from the soil; winds lash the trees. There
is no longer
Tranquilidad, pero una tierra del roto flamboyán.

And yet the travelers marvel at the beauty of Tabasco.
¿Cómo se llama esto? ¿Qué? ¿Un misterio sagrado?

Finale
[Summer, 1982]
Alexander Shacklebury

The sun's honeysuckle shower swarmed
Over green grass. The wind frolicked
In the fragrance in which it
Was born. Blossoms thronged and,
Like a droplet-kingdom, formed
Waves of color. Happiness kissed
The outdoors.

And I, I played indoors because
My mother was dying of cancer.

Toys were my friends, solemnly aligned,
Play-worn, but made
Silent companions.

***

I remember visiting my mother
With my father and infant brother.
The treatments were young, the science
Was young, and so was she.

I saw her in her chamber.
She was radioactive, and thus quarantined.
She would walk to us and
Press her hand against the glass.
I pressed my hand, against
The glass, to her hand, so that
We could touch.

***

Love and misery are twins:
They defile all barriers.

***

The judges are free to judge me:
Let them complain about
What I am, what I am not.

I can give but one thing:
A glimpse at what I write
And why I write
The way I do.

Ineptitude Slotted
Eugene Novogrodsky

I am seeing my universe.

Maybe.

But it's unsatisfactory, tawdry, hollow, a wisp . . .

The plumber splices a line.

He tells me to turn off the water.

I do.

The carpenter tells me to help lift a couch out of his
workspace.

I do.

Two simple jobs.

I return to my crumpled vision,

Telling myself my books are my soul - delusion -

As I wanted to do more, be more

Than a stumbling senior who turns off water and lifts a
couch . . .

Absolution
Weasel

our words were too small
for our hearts. our stories
merged and became
unmarried licenses spray-
painted around the bones of
our ring fingers. that
was all we could hope
for. matrimony is only
a god-given right.

i wrote our vows
in fire; wore the ashes
on my forehead to
absolve the sins of my
past life before we engraved
ourselves into each other.

when i proposed to you,
we were criminals tearing
at the nature of society. our
love was not human enough;
we were not human enough.

i never grew into the holiness
i had wanted to become. there
was still a guitar left burning
that i have yet to hear.

I took your hand and etched
these words onto your
heart because i still sweat
nightmares on the good days,
and you've been the only one
to soothe the grease from my
veins; to keep the dissonance alive.

Politics
Harold Rodinsky

Consensus, like fine cloth, an agreement between warp and
woof
for many different threads from different spinning
to lay together, creating a common image

cloth loosely woven, porous, allowing wind to waft through
made with a few thinner threads, presents form without
substance,
serves but does not last

tapestry tightly entwined provides and protects
many threads, stout and fine, holding firm against the
elements
a strong visage comprised of all the filaments

the winds of time and change blow strongly now
the tapestry I thought I wore, the once common image
dissolving into faded madras

as I stand here freezing

Brown Eyes
PW Covington

A lonely, brown-eyed child appears,
She clutches a Disney doll
And petitions me

With the eyes of Mogadishu
The eyes of Matagalpa

The eyes of Matamoros

Eyes too dry to cry
Eyes too tired to hope for more
Than survival

Hidden In The Light
Loretta Diane Walker

On the other side of that window ledge of light,
life, that hairy-foot mystery, attempts to hide its bulk
beneath the rumpled white sheet of morning.
Dust creeps up the pale walls, a conspirator in the plot.
It learned to hide like deceit, that quick-tongued chameleon.

I want my day to leap with simplicity,
but simplicity is a clever fish,
too swift to hook.
I am confined in this stark room
of complexities, staring at my numbered days.
Do I do laundry, gas the car before ice dresses
the streets with its slick coat
or plan a vacation I cannot afford?
Details that become blurred
when the double-barrel
of cancer is aimed at my breast.
When the buck shots of those cells splinter,
spread underneath my skin,
a surgeon cuts them out.
Her hands steady even though a week ago
she lost her husband in a cave of water.

My body drinks in cocktails of chemo,
burns from the thin red cross of radiation,
while I eat from a table of fear.
The same table where life,
that hairy-foot mystery, attempts to hide.
What foolishness!
Does it not know its extremities are exposed?
The smallest of its secrets too large to conceal?
With catlike caution, I amble towards its stillness.
Wait for its limp hand to move.
Wait for its next surprise.

Caravanserai
Müesser Yeniay

O the earth tribe
drums were played, doors were closed
in caravanserai

a candle, a loaf of bread, a dish of soup
and a sack of oat for the horse

in this courtyard shadowed by ever-present tree
mostly three days

then a caravan of three thousand camels . . .

on the wall an axe, a battle axe
bodies are hot by fireplace

and the moon grows as if it settles
a new daytime

Por Vida
Odilia Galván Rodríguez

paraísos

pequeños

partidos en trozos

como el papel picado

da forma a mundos

la poesía es

por vida

For Life

paradises

little ones

parceled up

as perforated paper

is cut to pieces

to shape worlds ~

poetry is

for life

Sonnet of Love
Lamar Jones

Honestly, love has its own dialect
Pulls heart strings in every direction
It's soluble in every aspect
Meticulous, random in selection
Bare knuckle brawler when love fists provoked
Emotional, up, back, roller coasters
Scientific method, prodded and poked
Hearts on sleeves, permanent fused memories
Remedies, it be telekinetic
Boundaries impossible to contain
Yet kind enough to mend broken pieces
Love has traveled far beyond the distant plains
Indeed love is worth all the sacrifice
True love makes tears soothe fire and soul like ice

Self-Identification Interrogation
Eloísa Pérez-Lozano

Your face is darker than mine
so you're already one step ahead of me,
fitting in more at this Latino gathering
as we meet for the first time.

"¿De dónde eres?"[1] you ask,
an innocent enough question
I ask of others all the time,
but one that makes me uneasy.

These are the words I hear:
"What family ancestry connects you to us?
What's your anchor, your link, your key?"

I'm already nervous,
afraid of not belonging, of your judgment
so I stumble on words
I've spoken my whole life:

*"Pues, yo soy nacida aquí
Pero mis papás son de México."*[2]

I make myself breathe,
my stilted speech not helping assuage
my fear of what you think of me,
whether or not you'll let me in...

Fortunately, you either don't notice
or give me the benefit of the doubt

You accept me and I mentally sigh in relief,
my confident Spanish now floating through the air,
interspersed with the ashes of my anxiety.

1 "Where are you from?"
2 "Well, I was born here, but my parents are from Mexico."

Dreaming With Emily
César Leonardo De León

There were birds
With raindrop wings
Strung like pearls
On violin strings

Purple canopies of hyacinth
Bending down to kiss the sea

An ant with an enormous seed
A clod of dirt, eternity, and Emily.

Recovery
Emily J. Foltz

Three sixty-five:
One day at a time
Feeling barely alive;
Seventy-eight beats per sixty,
Got to do this…get through this,
Can't stop now; nowhere to hide.

Look what you'd have missed
Had three one thirteen gone down--

Three sixty-five:
Now I know why
I want my life!
Seventy-eight beats per sixty,
Twenty/twenty ahead of me, happy, joyous and free,
One day at a time.

Red Ribbon Day: A Song for Kiki Camarena
Rickey E. Pittman

Today, I heard your story,
And my eyes were opened wide,
And though I never met you.
I know how hard you tried.

You exposed all the lies,
The payoffs and the greed,
To bring down los narcos,
And for that, they made you bleed.

Sometimes in the Valley,
A sad dark rooster cries,
Teaching us that it matters,
How you lived and how you died.

Now red ribbons tell your story,
And honor your memory,
One man can make a difference,
I know you did for me.

And the wind carries your ashes,
To the place where heroes go,
From the top of Signal Mountain,
To the borders of Old Mexico

Epilogue Of An Unpublished Chap Book
James Griswold

I've put my joys, my fears, my being,
scribbled in worn volumes,
placed on dusty high shelves,
in cobwebbed corners,
deep in the abyss of my soul.

Time to throw open the windows of the abyss,
dust off the volumes, turn the heavy laden pages
 and face the reflection of my life buried there.

MEET THE POETS

Alexander Shacklebury is an RGV poet who has been published in numerous journals and anthologies. Alexander provides a pessimistic worldview.

Ann Fogelman, a writer of memories in prose and poetry, lives in Friendswood, Texas. Her work appeared in *Boundless*, Texas Poetry Calendar, Pets Across America, The Noble Generation, That Thing You Do and Old Mountain Press Anthologies. Ann is a member of BAWL, Gulf Coast Poets, Poetry Society of Texas and OLLI at UTMB in Galveston.

Annika: Since 2008 I have participated in the German International Poetry Slam Championship five times and have advanced to the semi-finals twice. In 2012 I took part in the Slam at the Nuyorican Poets Café in New York City where I reached the top 5. In 2012 I was invited by the German Goethe-Institute to host the Poetry Slam-Championships in India. I am the founding member of two monthly literary events in Oldenburg (since 2011) and Bremen (since 2012) as well as the MC of the poetry Slam in Leer, Germany. Besides writing, I work as a high school teacher (subjects: English and German.)

Arturo Saldaña: A once quiet fire morphed into a blazing inferno. Life offers crisis and opportunity; wisdom is to know the difference. Border life offers two aspects of a single journey. My life has cleansed and annealed me; I stand stronger in the heat of battle and of love.

Aseneth Garza: Writing has been a healing and expressive process throughout my life. I write about personal issues and Latin America. I have done academic writing on Latin American politics and I hope to write in a legal setting. However, the style of writing that is most freeing is poetry.

Ashley Hodgson: I write sermons for my fellowship, mostly about the complexities of morality and a bit on world mythology.

Recently I've been focusing more on poetry and autobiographical work. I write to explore myself.

Beto Conde first wrote about Vietnam, one of twenty selected to read at the 25th anniversary of the VN wall in DC. He also writes about growing up and living in the dual cultures of south Texas. He published, *America Down By The River,* short stories and poems in 2011. He is one several co-founders of the Narciso Martínez Cultural Art Center Writers Forum.

César Leonardo De León is the 2014 VIPF Poetry Slam Champion. His poetry has been published in the anthologies *Juventud!: Growing up on the Border, Boundless 2013 and 2014,* among others, and most recently in *The Acentos Review.* In 2012 he received a Golden Circle Award from The University of Columbia Press, and in 2014 he was awarded 2nd place in poetry from the Texas Intercollegiate Press Association.

Charles McGregor is a twenty-six-year-old Florida native. Currently he is teaching at the University of Texas-Pan American while working on his MFA in Creative Writing. His poetry can be found in modest literary magazines such as *Xenith, Enhance, No Infinite, Boundless* and the *Portland Review.* Follow him on Twitter @CMcgregor209.

Chip Dameron has published six books of poetry, including *Waiting for an Etcher* (2015). His poems and essays have appeared in a variety of publications in the U.S. and abroad. He lives and writes in Brownsville.

Eduardo R. Vega: Originally from McAllen, Eduardo Vega has lived in San Antonio for most of the last 20 years. A career educator, his poetry focuses on food, Tejano culture, and social justice. When not writing at the neighborhood taquería, he's often found at various slams and open mics in San Antonio.

Eloísa Pérez-Lozano was selected to be a Juried Poet during the 2014 Houston Poetry Fest and her poetry has been featured in *The Bayou Review, Illya's Honey, The Acentos Review, The Ofi Press,* and the Johnson County Library's 2014 Poem-a-Day Program, among others.

Eugene "Gene" Novogrodsky of Brownsville has written slices of life (and more) for nearly 15 years. He is a founding member of the Narciso Martinez Cultural Arts Center Writers Forum in San Benito.

Harold Rodinsky is currently employed as a professor of psychology in Biological Psychology and the Biology of Learning, Memory, and Cognition at a university in San Antonio, Texas. He has been writing for more than 50 years and lists among his early influences: Gary Snyder, Kenneth Rexroth and Lawrence Ferlinghetti all of whom he was acquainted with in San Francisco in the 1960's. His recent work includes poems published in *Quirk* (2011, 2012, 2013, 2014), an annual literary journal published by the UIW Press and by *Voices de la Luna* (2013, 2014, 2015).

Homer Starkey is a graduate of the University of Houston Creative Writing Program and the author of the novel *You Will Believe in Love.* When not writing poetry and fiction he embarks on many an armchair adventure, runs on the hard concrete streets of Houston, or discovers the curious habits of ocean life with his five-year-old son.

Jane "The Rev" Wenninger turned to poetry after retirement to mingle with writers and to further explore the twists, turns, humor, and depth of being thoughtful, spiritual, feeling and funny human beings. Too numerous to mention here, her work has appeared in over twenty publications ranging from local to international.

Jeannette Moreno McNeill: I am a Mexican board-certified psychiatrist and psychoanalyst, who recently got her American citizenship and moved to McAllen. When I tried to get a job here, I was told I was "overqualified." I now walk across the bridge to give consultations to the few the happy music and drinks haven't gotten to first. I have written published papers. One, "Migration and Suicide" was presented at the World Congress of Emergency

Psychiatry in Italy. My written thesis for becoming a psychoanalyst was "A sense of humor in the healing process." I am new at poetry.

Jim Griswold, a Chicago native, has published many poems in online venues, as well as in the *Longfellow Chronicles*. He has been published in Boundless 2013 and 2014. His poem Cries of Honor is on display at the Iwo Jima Monument Museum in Harlingen Texas. He uses song, poetry and performance art in his life-long vocation as a teacher.

JoAnn DeLuna is a Texican, bilingual poet and journalist living in New York. Her poetry has been published in anthologies in New York and Texas. She regularly performs throughout NYC in events combining multiple art forms. She received her journalism MA from City University London.

Joanne Uppendahl, author of *She Who Gathers Stones*, published in *Astropoetica; Hubble Heritage Arts; Triggerfish Critical Review;* Fortunate Childe Anthologies: *Lilith; Postcards from Eve; Tipping the Sacred Cow* and *Vintage; Boundless 2012, 2013, and 2014 Anthologies. She received a Pushcart nomination for Flying into the Sun by El Zarape Press*

José Rafael Castilleja, a writer, a poet, an engineer, and a community leader. He has written technical articles, poems for local journals and detail descriptions of local events for the local newspapers. He was born and raised in the Rio Grande Valley and has worked in Texas and California.

Joyce Gullickson is a Registered Nurse and poet living in Georgetown, Texas. She co-hosts the Annual Georgetown Poetry Festival, in an attempt to bring poetry to the people, and give local poets an opportunity to join together in friendship. Her motto is "Have Poems, Will Travel."

Julieta Corpus writes obsessively, compulsively, and desperately . . . so that she doesn't scream.

Katherine Hoerth is the author two poetry collections, *Goddess Wears Cowboy Boots* (Lamar University Press, 2014) and *The Garden Uprooted*. She received the 2014 Helen Smith Memorial Prize for the Best Book of Poetry from the Texas Institute of Letters. Katherine teaches writing at the University of Texas Pan American.

Kathy Trenfield Raines, an English teacher at Los Fresnos High School in Texas, has enjoyed writing and teaching composition and literature for over thirty years. She has written since childhood but got a jump start through the New Jersey and National Writing Projects in the 1990s. She enjoys writing essays and stories as well as poetry and has been published in *Boundless, Escuchame, Voices From the Chicho* and *Along the River* 2. Also, she loves acting, exploring nature, reading, playing music, and visiting with friends, family, and pets.

Kjell Nykvist is an RGV poet who has been published in numerous journals and anthologies. Kjell provides an optimistic worldview.

Lamar Jones Lamar Jones was born in Camden, NJ and raised in South Florida where he discovered that writing was his escape from the troubles of his world. He strives to positively impact a multitude of people and be a better man than he was yesterday. www.LamarJones.com

Laura Peña was born and raised in Houston. She holds a BA in English Literature and an MA in Education. She is a bilingual elementary school teacher and has been published in *di-vêrsé-city*, Boundless, Houston Poetry Fest anthology, The Bayou Review, Harbinger Asylum, Illya's Honey, The Red River Review, and The Texas Poetry Calendar. Laura has read in venues around Houston and Austin and is past president and current recording secretary of Gulf Coast Poets, is a member of The Poetry Society of Texas, Academy of American Poets, and The Writer's League of Texas. Laura organizes Poetry Out of Bounds each year for Houston Poetry Fest.

Linda Romero is from Harlingen, Texas. She has been published in the VIPF *Boundless* anthologies since 2010, *Along the River 2: More Voices from the Rio Grande* (VAO Publishing), and *Twenty: In Memoriam* (El Zarape Press). She serves as coordinator for Vidas Cruzadas, a creative writing mentoring program for Life Center. She is also co-editor for *Left Hand of the Father*, an online literary journal. Linda is currently working on her MFA in Creative Writing at UT-Pan American.

Lisa Adam works as a museum curator, and, by extension, writes poetry to curate--select, arrange, and preserve--various experiences from the natural and human world that she hopes will resonate with visitors to her writing. She has previously published essays or poetry in Nature Conservancy Magazine, The Christian Science Monitor, and several print and online journals.

Loretta Diane Walker, a multiple Pushcart nominee, has published two collections of poetry and her manuscript *In This House* is forth coming in 2015. Her manuscript *Word Ghetto* won the 2011 Bluelight Press Book Award. She teaches music in Odessa, Texas. Loretta received a BME from Texas Tech University and earned a MA from the University of Texas of the Permian Basin.

Lucinda Zamora-Wiley is originally from San Antonio, Texas, but she has called the Rio Grande Valley home for twenty years now. She is a passionate high school English teacher in South Texas ISD and a student of life, currently pursuing an MFA in Creative Writing at University of Texas Pan-American. She is a lover of art and writing ekphrastic poetry. In the coming year, it is her goal to publish a chapbook of poetry as her MFA thesis.

LuLynne Streeter's poems, short stories, and essays have appeared in Chaparral Poetry Forum, Texas Poetry Calendar, Houston Chronicle, New Mexico Magazine and other regional publications. Her chapbook "Dry Borders" was published by Hollering Woman Press. She has traveled throughout the U.S. and Mexico and lives on Galveston Island.

Mario Mansilla Moya lives in Mexico City, where he is a law student.

Mateo Mansilla Moya is a 20-year-old Mexican citizen living in Mexico City, where he is a law student. He likes writing poetry, stories, and essays. His writing has been published in the U.S.A., Mexico, and Germany in magazines and anthologies. His work is being sold online and is available at bookstores in the European Union and GooglePlay. He recently published a law book.

Meliton Hinojosa is a Chicano poet, period.

Mike Gullickson is co-editor of The Enigmatist and Blue Hole Magazines, as well as co-chairman of the Annual Georgetown Poetry Festival. His book The Promise of Music is available on Amazon. He reads at various venues around the country, and was the 2008 National Senior Poet Laureate.

Müesser Yeniay was born in İzmir in 1984; she graduated from Ege University, with a degree in English Language and Literature. She got her M.A in Turkish Literature from Bilkent University. She has won several prizes in Turkey including Yunus Emre (2006), Homeros Attila İlhan (2007), Ali Riza Ertan (2009), Enver Gökçe (2013) poetry prizes. She was also nominated for the Pushcart Prize by Muse Pie Press in the U.S.A.

Nephtalí De León is known primarily for his poetry, children's stories, and essays. He illustrates most of his books. He has been published in Mexico, France, the U.S., and Spain, with his writings have been translated into several languages, such as Russian, Chinese, Arabic, and Vietnamese. His website is http://Nephtali.Net.

Nianna E. Gustovich is a French and Spanish teacher at Valley View High School who began writing short stories and poetry at the age of 10. She worked as a news correspondent for the Tribune Chronicle in Warren, Ohio in the early 1990's and has been reading her latest works with the poets from Pasta, Poetry, and Vino and introduced Shit Therapy to the Rio Grande Valley at 100

Thousand Poets For Change in 2014.

Odilia Galván Rodríguez, eco-poet, writer, editor, and activist, is the author of four volumes of poetry, her latest, *Red Earth Calling: ~cantos for the 21st Century~*. She's worked as an editor for Matrix Women's News Magazine, Community Mural's Magazine, and most recently at Tricontinental Magazine in Havana, Cuba. She facilitates creative writing workshops nationally, and moderates: *Poets Responding to SB 1070*, and *Love and Prayers for Fukushima*, both Facebook pages dedicated to bringing attention to social justice issues, which affect the lives and wellbeing of many people. Her poetry appears in numerous anthologies and literary journals on and offline.

Oscar C. Peña has been a juried poet at *Houston Poetry Fest* and has been published in the Austin International Poetry Festival anthology *di-vêrsé-city*, Rio Grande Valley International Poetry Festival anthology *Boundless*; and the San Antonio Poetry Fair anthology *Voices Along the River*. He was on the Houston 2012, 2013 & 2014 *Word Around Town* poetry tours. Oscar's poetry has also been published in the San Pedro River Review and he has presented his work to high school and college students and performed his poetry at venues throughout Texas.

PW Covington has been a fixture in the Texas Indie Lit scene for almost 20 years. Covington has written two collections of poetry and a novel, and his work has been included in projects published by South Texas College, UTPA, and Our lady of the Lake University. His next poetry collection is to be published by Slough Press and will be available in 2015. PW Covington is a 100% service connected disabled veteran and a convicted felon.

Richard Sánchez is a creative writer from Edinburg, Texas and a graduate of Pan American University. His work has been published in Valley Song, Texas Trophy Hunters Magazine, *Somos Primos* (Albuquerque, NM) , and Interstice (South Texas College). His most recent book, The Jelly Jar, is now available at the Museum of South Texas History and Paragraphs On Padre (SPI).

Rickey E. Pittman is a poet.

Saraí García has been writing for years. Recently she has realized writing is more therapeutic than just being called a hobby. She holds an MA with an English focus.

Seres J. Magana is a student at UTPA. He is an aspiring writer. He lives in McAllen, Texas.

Shawna Kennedy is an MFA in Creative Writing student, at the University of Texas RGV. She worked on *Riversedge*, UTRGV's literary magazine, as an assistant to the Editor-in -Chief for the 2014 issue. She currently works with the TLI program in the Valley, promoting reading and writing in secondary schools.

Shirley Rickett retired to the Valley in 2005. She holds an MA in Education and in English from the University of Missouri-Kansas City. Her poems have appeared in over thirty journals and magazines, and she has authored three chapbooks. Her work won first prize in the McAllen Green Living contest and some of her work has been nominated for a Pushcart Prize. Her full-length book of poems, *Transplant*, is forthcoming from FlowerSong Books.

Sophia: I live and am a poet in China. I love reading and writing. I can write Chinese traditional poetry and also modern poems. I would like to share every thought-flower with others. The reason why I would love to devote into writing is that saving those people who have suffered a lot of misery and I also would love to share every secret with my reader. Nephtali De Leon is my teacher. I am his favorite student. We are cooperating our poetry (Kiss'in Rift Valley). The poetry will publish soon, and a novel (Love Between Sunrise And Moonset.)

Terry Jude Miller is a poet from Houston. A Juried Poet of the 2011/2012 Houston Poetry Festivals, his work is published in scores of publications including the Texas Poetry Calendar, Foundling Review, Boston Literary Magazine, and the Birmingham Arts Journal. He is the creator of the Texas Poets

Podcast.

Trevor Wainwright This year will be Trev's 4th consecutive appearance at the VIPF. On his last tour he brought his total of tour poems to 575, many written entirely on inspiration on the spot, including one about his plane trying to land in the fog as events unfolded. He will again have taken in other festivals and events and worked voluntary at an animal rescue center, before arriving at the VIPF and have written even more poems. He puts his prolificness down to the fact that when he is over here he has the time to fully concentrate on his poetry.

Viktoria Valenzuela is a writer living in San Antonio, Texas. She has been published in various journals around the U.S.A. and once in Australia. She has performed dramatic readings of her work at Our Lady of the Lake University, Luminaria, SUNY Oswego, and The Sterling Nature Center. Valenzuela holds a BA in Creative Writing from the University of New York at Oswego.

Vincent Cooper is a poet living in San Antonio, TX. He is the author of, "Where The Reckless Ones Come to Die," a chapbook released by Aztlan Libre Press in September 2014. Cooper has been published in several zines and journals in South Texas. His writing is based on family and life in the barrio.

Walter Birdwell travels the old but obscure paths with his soulmate Yolanda. He gathers his material while he wanders these paths. Others will discover them sooner or later.

Weasel is a writer and founder of the magazines Vagabonds and The Haunted Traveler. When he's away from work he spends most of his free time managing a small publisher called Weasel Press. You can discover more of Weasel's work at the website provided. http://hitchingpoets.wix.com/poetweasel

We bring fresh voices to the literary conversation.

Since 2008, we are a proud sponsor of the Rio Grande Valley International Poetry Festival and we are proud to bring you *Boundless*.

Rio Grande Valley International Poetry Festival
www.valleypoetryfest.org

Boundless is the official anthology of the Rio Grande Valley International Poetry Festival (V.I.P.F.), founded in 2008 by Daniel García Ordaz and Brenda Nettles Riojas. V.I.P.F. is a held annually on the last weekend in April in deep South Texas in celebration of National Poetry Month, with concurrent readings in the United States and Mexico.

V.I.P.F. is a program of Art That Heals, Inc.

MORE BOOKS FROM EL ZARAPE PRESS

Beautiful Scars and *Insomnia* by Edward Vidaurre

*You Know What I'm Sayin'? (Poetry*Drama)* by Daniel García Ordaz

a celebration of the common experience of language and culture

ISBN-10: 0978995414

Twenty: In Memoriam (by several poets from across the U.S.)

in response to the school shootings at Sandy Hook Elem., in Newtown, CT, on 12/14/ 2012
ISBN-10: 1494326752

Boundless: The Anthology of the Rio Grande Valley Int'l. Poetry Festival

Published annually by El Zarape Press, proud sponsor of V.I.P.F.

www.valleypoetryfest.org

Dear Reader!

Thank you for reading our collection of poetry! Now that you've finished our latest offering to the poetry gods, we'd love to get your feedback through an honest review at amazon.com and goodreads.com, ibooks, etc., as well as any other literary site you visit. Video reviews would be cool too!

V.I.P.F. offers anthology submissions to all interested poets—not only those who've registered with us. For more details about our festival, visit www.valleypoetryfest.org.

Please let us know about your poetry news on Facebook: https://www.facebook.com/groups/rgvipf/. Please e-mail VIPF at rgvipf@hotmail.com when your review is posted or if you have questions about our festival: always held the last weekend in April.

Sincerely,

Daniel and Brenda, Founders.

www.ingramcontent.com/pod-product-compliance
Lightning Source LLC
Chambersburg PA
CBHW031338060726
47590CB00007B/2524